**The Driver and the Investor:
A Story of Wealth and Wisdom**
Book #1: Starting the Journey

Copyright © 2024 by Rhett Winfield

All rights reserved.

No part of this book may be reproduced, distributed, or transmitted in any form or by any means, including photocopying, recording, or other electronic or mechanical methods, without the prior written permission of the publisher, except in the case of brief quotations embodied in critical reviews and certain other noncommercial uses permitted by copyright law. For permission requests, contact the publisher at the address below.

This is a work of fiction. Names, characters, businesses, places, events, and incidents are either the product of the author's imagination or used in a fictitious manner. Any resemblance to actual persons, living or dead, or actual events is purely coincidental.

For information, address inquiries to:
rhettwinfield.com

— Legal Disclaimer —

The information in this book, **The Investor and the Driver: A Story of Wealth and Wisdom (Book #1: Starting the Journey)**, is presented for **entertainment and educational purposes only**. The ideas, strategies, and tips shared here are based on personal experience and research, but they should not be taken as financial, legal, or investment advice. Always do your own research and talk to a qualified financial expert, lawyer, or tax advisor before making any investment decisions.

The names, characters, businesses, places, and events in this book are **completely fictional**. Any similarities to real people, places, or situations are just coincidences. The examples and stories are used to explain ideas and should not be assumed to represent real-life situations.

The author and publisher do not guarantee the accuracy, usefulness, or completeness of the information in this book. They are not responsible for any errors or missing details, or for any outcomes that result from using the information.

Investing in tax liens and real estate carries risk, and past success does not guarantee future results. Always do your own research and seek help from professionals before making decisions with your money.

This book does not promise financial success or freedom. It is provided "as is," with no guarantees. The author and publisher are not responsible for any decisions, damages, or issues that may come from using the information contained in this book. Always **consult a financial professional** prior to making any investment choices.

— Preface —

Book #1:
Starting the Journey

Imagine a chance encounter that changes the course of your life. You're on a routine day, doing your job, and then—out of nowhere—you meet someone who opens a door to an entirely new world. That's how this story began.

For Marcus, it was an ordinary day behind the wheel, driving for a rideshare company, until he overheard a conversation that piqued his curiosity. The topic? Tax lien investing—a world he had never considered. Little did he know that this fleeting moment would spark a journey, one that would lead him from that driver's seat to the helm of his own financial empire.

The Investor and the Driver (Book #1) is not just a story about tax liens; it's about seizing opportunities, learning from mentors, and realizing that success comes to those who are open to new possibilities. As you read Marcus's journey, you'll learn the ins and outs of tax lien investing—how it works, why it works, and most importantly, how it can work for you.

The world of tax liens may seem complex or intimidating at first, but through this book, you'll see how anyone, regardless of their background, can learn the ropes and start building real wealth. Marcus's story is proof that with the right guidance and a willingness to learn, financial freedom is within reach.

Let this book serve as your guide, as Marcus's mentor once served for him. Whether you're just curious about tax liens or ready to jump in, the key is to take that first step—just as Marcus did after that chance encounter.

— Prologue —

A Drive to the Airport

The hum of the rideshare car's engine faded into the background as the man leaned back into the plush leather seat. "No, just reinvest the redemption earnings into the next auction. We'll see the interest stack up again," his voice carried confidence as he wrapped up the call. Glancing briefly out the window, he took in the sun-drenched streets of Beverly Hills, weaving seamlessly into the conversation. "Yeah, the numbers are looking good, I'm not worried. We've already got our eye on the next property in Fulton County. Okay, I'll touch base when I land."

He ended the call by tapping the screen, put his phone in his laptop case's side pocket, and turned his attention to the driver.

"Thanks for picking me up. LAX, right?"

"Yes, sir." The driver nodded curiously after hearing the investor's conversation.

As the man opened his laptop, the glow of the screen casting a faint light in the backseat, the driver couldn't resist. "Sounds like you're into real estate? Investing in properties?"

The investor chuckled, his fingers briefly pausing on the keyboard. "Sort of. More like investing in tax lien certificates. It's a bit different from buying and flipping houses, but it's all about strategy."

The driver was intrigued when he looked at him through the rearview mirror. "Tax liens? Never heard of those being such a big deal."

"Well, that's the thing," the investor began, leaning forward slightly. "Most people don't realize the potential. Tax liens give you the chance to earn interest returns that blow savings accounts out of the water—or even acquire properties for a fraction of their value through foreclosure. But you've got to know how to work the system."

The driver's curiosity was piqued. "So how does it work? You're basically waiting for someone to lose their property?"

"Not exactly," the investor smiled, appreciating the driver's directness. "When someone doesn't pay their property taxes, the county sells a lien on their property to an investor like me. The property owner can pay off the taxes—plus interest—or if they don't, I might end up with the property. The trick is in knowing which liens to buy, which states to focus on, and how to manage the process."

"So, it's like investing in someone else's debt?" The driver's brow furrowed as he navigated the busy LA traffic.

"In a way, yes, but it's backed by real property," the investor explained, glancing at his laptop screen, now pulling up a report from a recent auction in Indiana. "Think of it like this: even if the homeowner redeems the lien by paying their taxes, I still walk away with a nice return—sometimes as high as 16% or more. If they don't redeem, I get the property for the cost of the unpaid taxes."

Impressed, the driver whistled a high pitch that bent down in amazement. "Sounds risky, though. What if the property's a wreck?"

The investor nodded thoughtfully, appreciating the skepticism. "There's risk, sure. But with the right research, due diligence, and a focus on low-competition states and counties, you can minimize that risk. For example, you might consider investing in countries with shorter redemption periods. Properties here are more likely to foreclose. That's where the real strategy comes in."

The highway stretched ahead toward the airport. There was a brief moment of silence from the driver. Finally, he asked, "So how'd you get into it?"

The investor leaned back, a small smile on his face. "I was just like you—curious. Heard someone talking about it at an event years ago. Then I did my research, made my first investment, and... well, let's just say I've been flying out to different tax lien auctions ever since."

The conversation paused as they approached the LAX terminal, the hustle and bustle of travelers and departing flights just ahead. The driver glanced in the mirror again. "Maybe I'll look into it. Sounds like there's more to it than I thought."

The investor gave a final nod as he closed his laptop. "You should. It's not about getting rich quick; it's about playing the long game. But if you do it right, tax liens can be one of the smartest investments you'll ever make."

With that, the car slowed to a stop, and the investor reached for his luggage. "Good luck out there," the driver said as he waved him off, already thinking about what he'd just learned.

And as the investor walked toward the terminal, ready to catch his flight to the next opportunity, one thing was clear: tax lien investing was his game, and he'd mastered it. Now, it was time for others to learn the ropes.

This book would show them how.

— Introduction —

Building Wealth
(One Investment at a Time)

Imagine a world where your investments consistently generate double-digit returns, where your money works for you and, in some cases, even puts you on the path to property ownership. This is the potential of **tax lien investing**. It's not a get-rich-quick scheme; it's a smart, deliberate strategy that, when done right, can build significant wealth over time.

In the pages that follow, you'll be taken on a journey—a journey where the complexities of tax lien investing will be simplified, and where the path to success will be laid out step by step. Whether you're completely new to tax liens or have dabbled in real estate before, this book will serve as your guide to mastering the art and science of tax lien certificates.

But this isn't just a book filled with facts and figures. It's also a story—a story of a chance encounter between an investor and a rideshare driver, both on different paths but destined to learn from one another. Through their conversations, you'll learn about the core concepts of tax lien investing, and by the end of their journey, you too will have the knowledge needed to invest confidently and strategically.

Why Tax Lien Investing?

Tax lien investing is unique. It's an investment backed by real property, often with high returns and, depending on the state, a relatively low-risk profile. At its core, tax lien investing involves buying the right to collect unpaid property taxes, and in return, you earn interest on that debt. If the property owner doesn't pay their taxes, you may have the opportunity to foreclose on the property itself—acquiring real estate for a fraction of its value.

With interest rates often ranging from 10% to 18% (sometimes higher in special cases), tax liens offer a far more attractive return than traditional savings accounts, bonds, or CDs. Plus, if a property owner fails to redeem the lien, you may find yourself the owner of a valuable asset. But make no mistake—this is not a "hands-off" investment. Success in tax liens requires research, patience, and strategy.

Introducing...
The Investor and the Driver
A Story of Wealth and Wisdom

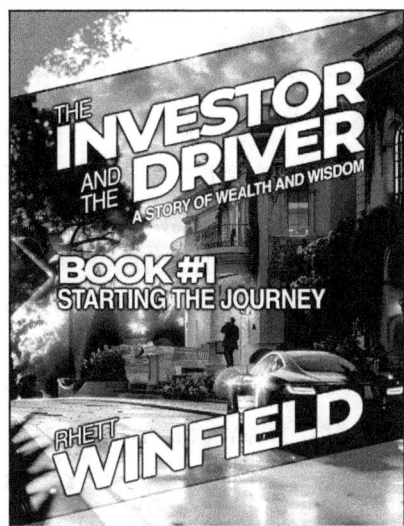

Book #1:
Starting the Journey

A successful investor needs to catch his next flight, so he requests a ride to the airport on his ride-share app. He's on the phone when he gets into the car, and the driver can't help but overhear the conversation.

Book #2:
Facing Challenges

James is the investor in our story who Marcus meets at the beginning. But James becomes much more than a successful investor when he decides to teach Marcus. He becomes a mentor. Everyone faces challenges, but this book is about the importance of having a wise and accessible mentor who truly helps you. James is that mentor in this story.

Book #3:
Bigger Risks, Bigger Rewards

Marcus, the driver at the beginning of the story in Book 1, is now a successful investor. He has learned his lessons well, and he has grown as a person. Book 3 brings him full circle in a way that will have you cheering for him because there will be a surprise realization and a new role for him at the end.

A Quick Overview

Here's a quick overview of this three-book series...

The Investor and the Driver follows the journey of Marcus, a rideshare driver, and James, a seasoned investor, as they navigate the world of tax lien investing.

In **Book #1: Starting the Journey**, Marcus is introduced to the opportunities within tax lien investing through a chance encounter with James. As their mentorship deepens, Marcus begins to understand the basic strategies and potential of this investment vehicle. With James's guidance, Marcus takes his first steps toward financial freedom, learning about the true profit potential of tax liens and the importance of strategy.

Book #2: Facing Challenges takes Marcus deeper into the complexities of tax lien investing. As he encounters new obstacles—both ethical and practical—Marcus grapples with the moral implications of acquiring properties through foreclosures and confronts unexpected hurdles in the investment process. His mentor, James, helps him navigate these pitfalls while pushing Marcus to strengthen his strategies and expand his knowledge. This volume highlights the difficulties that arise when investments don't go as planned, and the perseverance required to stay focused.

In **Book #3: Bigger Risks, Bigger Rewards**, Marcus takes on even more significant opportunities, scaling up his investments while facing the allure of other "shiny" opportunities. With the stakes higher than ever, Marcus remains committed to his tax lien investment strategy, learning to balance risk and reward while continuing to revitalize communities. By the end, he reflects on the full arc of his journey, realizing not only the personal gains from his investments but also the broader impact he's made on others' lives.

Who Is This Book Series For?

Aspiring Investors: If you're looking to get started with a limited budget but want significant returns, tax lien investing is ideal. This book will show you how to start small and grow gradually.

Real Estate Enthusiasts: If you already have experience in real estate but want to diversify your portfolio, tax lien certificates can provide a steady stream of income with the potential for acquiring properties.

Curious Minds: If you've heard about tax liens but aren't sure how they work or whether they're worth pursuing, this book will provide clarity and direction.

The Goal

The goal of this series is to empower you with knowledge through an inspirational and informative story. By the time you finish reading this book, you'll not only understand how tax liens work, but you'll also have the confidence to dive in and make your first investment—just like the driver who became an investor himself.

So, buckle up.

You're about to learn how to build wealth, one investment at a time.

— Chapter 1 —

The Unexpected Lesson

The hum of engines and the shuffle of travelers at LAX provided a familiar soundtrack as the driver glanced at his next pick-up notification on the rideshare app. The name looked oddly familiar, but he couldn't quite place it. He made his way through the maze of terminals, finally pulling up to the designated spot. As the automatic doors slid open, he couldn't believe his eyes.

It was him—the same man he had driven to the airport a few days earlier. The one who had been on the phone, talking about tax liens.

The man, dressed in a sharp suit and rolling a carry-on behind him, spotted the car and raised his hand in recognition. As he slid into the back seat, they locked eyes in the rearview mirror. "Well, what are the odds?" the driver said, half-laughing at the coincidence.

The investor grinned. "I was just thinking the same thing." He buckled his seatbelt and placed his laptop case next to him, eyeing the driver curiously. "You were the one who drove me to the airport, right?"

The driver nodded. "Yeah, small world, huh?"

For a moment, the two men sat in silence as the car eased into traffic. The driver's curiosity, however, wouldn't let him stay quiet for long. "You know, when I dropped you off last time, I couldn't stop thinking about what you were saying on the phone—something about tax liens?"

The investor looked amused, but interested. "That's right. Did it catch your attention?"

"More than you'd think," the driver admitted. "I couldn't get it out of my head. You made it sound like there's real money in it."

"There is," the investor said, with a smile. "In fact, I just got back from attending a tax lien auction. It went well—picked up a few more certificates."

The driver nodded, intrigued. He'd been thinking about it ever since their last conversation, but he didn't know how to bring it up before. Now, with this bizarre coincidence, he felt like maybe it was meant to be. "I don't want to be that guy, but... do you think someone like me could get into it?"

The investor leaned forward slightly, clearly interested in where the conversation was heading. "You'd be surprised," he said. "I started small. Just a few hundred bucks on my first lien. You don't need to be rich to start. It's more about understanding the process."

The driver let out a small laugh, shaking his head. "It's crazy that we ran into each other again. I don't believe in coincidences like this."

"Neither do I," the investor replied, his tone more serious now. "Maybe it's a sign. You said you were interested, right?"

The driver nodded. "Yeah, I am. But I don't know where to begin."

"Well, how about this?" The investor pulled a business card from his laptop case and handed it over. "Give me a call sometime. I can walk you through the basics and show you what to look for. It's not as hard as people think. But it does take patience and strategy."

The driver took the card, feeling a surge of excitement. He'd never thought about tax liens before that first conversation, but now, it seemed like the opportunity was practically landing in his lap. "Are you serious? You'd really teach me?"

The investor nodded, settling back into his seat. "Sure. Everyone needs a starting point. And from the looks of it, you're ready to learn."

The car continued its journey through the congested freeway, but the air between them felt electric with possibility. As they neared the driver's exit, the investor extended his hand. "By the way, I'm James."

The driver shook his hand, smiling. "Nice to meet you, James. I'm Marcus."

They exchanged contact information, both men now aware that this wasn't just a random encounter—it was the start of something bigger. For Marcus, it was the chance to turn his curiosity into a reality, and for James, it was the opportunity to mentor someone who seemed genuinely eager to learn.

As the car pulled up to James' final destination, Marcus couldn't help but smile. "I'll be in touch, James."

"I'm looking forward to it, Marcus," James replied, stepping out of the car. "You might be surprised at where this journey takes you."

As Marcus drove away, card still in hand, he knew this was no coincidence. This was his chance.

Three Days Later...

Marcus sat at his small kitchen table, his phone resting beside him, waiting for James to call. Since their second meeting, Marcus hadn't been able to stop thinking about tax lien investing. The whole concept was foreign to him, but it also felt like an opportunity he couldn't ignore.

When his phone finally buzzed, Marcus answered immediately. "Hey, James," he said, trying to hide the anticipation in his voice.

"Hey Marcus, ready for your first lesson in tax liens?"

"Absolutely," Marcus replied, eager to get started.

"Great," James said, his tone upbeat. "Let's start with the big picture—what I like to call the perfect world scenario of tax lien investing. You've probably heard stories of people making incredible returns on their investments, right? Well, tax lien investing can be just as rewarding, but it's not always talked about. So, let me walk you through what's possible when everything goes right."

Marcus listened intently as James laid out the process.

The Basics: How It Works

James began explaining the core of tax lien investing. "When a property owner fails to pay their taxes, the local government still needs that money to function. So, they auction off a lien on the property to investors like us. The investor covers the unpaid taxes, and in exchange, the property owner has to pay back that amount plus interest—usually a pretty attractive rate."

"What's the interest like?" Marcus asked, trying to imagine how this could outpace other investments.

"In states like Florida and Illinois, the interest can go up to 18% or even higher," James explained. "It beats the return you'd get on a savings account, that's for sure. And the beauty is, you're basically guaranteed that return because the lien is backed by the property itself."

Marcus was beginning to see the appeal. "So, what happens if the property owner can't pay?"

"That's where things get really interesting," James said, pausing for effect. "If the owner doesn't redeem the lien by paying off the taxes plus interest, you can foreclose on the property and take ownership. And here's the kicker—you get it for the cost of the unpaid taxes, which is usually a fraction of the property's market value."

The Perfect World Scenario: High Returns, Low Risk

James continued, "Now, imagine this: you invest in a tax lien for a property worth $200,000, but the owner has only fallen behind on $5,000 in property taxes. You buy the lien, and the owner has a set period—called the redemption period—to pay you back with interest. Let's say the interest rate is 16%. If the owner redeems the lien after a year, you'll get your $5,000 back, plus $800 in interest. That's a nice return for just one lien."

Marcus nodded as James painted the picture. "But here's the perfect world scenario: the owner doesn't redeem the lien, and now you have the right to foreclose on the property. You can legally take ownership of that $200,000 house for just the $5,000 you invested. Now you've got a property that's worth 40 times your original investment."

"Wow," Marcus muttered, almost disbelieving.

James chuckled. "Yeah, it's a pretty sweet deal. But remember, this is the ideal outcome—where everything goes right. You either make solid interest on your investment, or you acquire a valuable piece of real estate. And if you play your cards right, you can reinvest those returns into more liens, building your wealth over time."

Reinvesting: The Key to Long-Term Success

"So, how do you make sure you keep building?" Marcus asked, thinking ahead.

"That's the beauty of tax lien investing," James said. "You can start small, and as you earn returns from redeemed liens, you reinvest those profits into more liens. Over time, this compounding effect grows your portfolio. Some investors are able to buy multiple properties this way, and all it takes is patience and smart reinvesting."

Marcus was impressed. He had heard about the importance of reinvesting before, but this seemed like a more direct way to grow wealth. "It sounds too good to be true," he admitted.

James didn't miss a beat. "It can be, if you don't do your homework. That's why due diligence is so important—researching the property before buying a lien, understanding the market, and knowing the state's laws. But if you stick to the basics and avoid the common pitfalls, you can do very well."

Potential Pitfalls: What to Watch Out For

James cautioned Marcus not to get too carried away by the perfect scenario. "Here's the reality: while tax lien investing can be extremely rewarding, it's not without its risks. Not every lien will result in foreclosure, and not every property is worth owning. Some may have title issues, or the property could be in disrepair. That's why you have to do your homework before jumping in."

Marcus jotted down notes, feeling both excited and slightly overwhelmed. "So what's the next step?"

James smiled on the other end of the line. "Next, we'll talk about how to get started with your first tax lien. But remember this: the perfect world scenario is real—you just have to be smart about how you get there."

— Chapter 2 —

A Perfect World Scenario: The True Profit Potential of Tax Lien Investing

Imagine stepping into the world of tax lien certificate investing with the perfect strategy, perfect timing, and perfect properties. Everything falls into place, and you experience firsthand the high returns, the excitement of winning at auction, and the thrill of watching your investment grow—without the headaches of complications. In this **perfect world scenario**, you, as the tax lien investor, maximize profits with minimal effort, setting the stage for financial success.

Step 1: Identifying the Golden Opportunity

It starts with your careful research. You've pinpointed a county that holds regular tax lien auctions with **consistent historical returns** and a **robust real estate market.** The property that you are currently examining belongs to a homeowner who has failed to make their property tax payments. Nonetheless, the property is still in excellent condition and situated in a burgeoning neighborhood with rising property values.

- The assessed property value is **$350,000**, yet the delinquent taxes amount to only **$7,500**.
- **It's a prime location:** high demand, excellent resale potential, and an area where property values have increased 10% annually.

You check for other liens or encumbrances on the property and discover that there are none. No IRS liens, no mortgages—just a clean tax lien waiting for you to claim.

Step 2: The Auction Triumph

On auction day, you're fully prepared. You've set clear **bidding limits** to avoid overpaying, but you're confident because you've done your homework. The auction begins, and there's minimal competition for your target property.

- The bidding starts at **18% interest**, but you're willing to go down to **10%** for this golden opportunity.
- After just a few rounds, the final bid is locked in at **12%**—and it's yours!

You've secured the lien with a 12% annual return, on a property that's almost certain to redeem. You've paid **$7,500** for the lien, and you can already envision the payoff.

Step 3: The Redemption Payoff

Months later, the redemption notice comes in. The homeowner, realizing their property is at risk, redeems the lien. You are paid **the full $7,500 back**, plus **12% interest**. This amounts to an additional **$900 in pure profit**—just for holding the lien for less than a year.

In this perfect scenario, you didn't have to lift a finger after the auction. No foreclosure, no property management—just a smooth, hassle-free return on your investment.

Step 4: Reaping the Foreclosure Reward

But what if the homeowner **doesn't redeem**? In this ideal scenario, even that works out in your favor. The redemption period ends, and the property becomes yours through foreclosure. Since you hold the senior lien, the property title transfers cleanly into your name.

Now you own a $350,000 property that you've acquired for just $7,500 in unpaid taxes. You hire a local real estate agent to assess the market, and after just a couple of minor repairs, the property is ready to hit the market.

- You list the property for **$360,000**, given that real estate in the area has appreciated over the past year.
- Within a few weeks, a buyer offers you **$355,000**—an incredible return on an investment that started with just **$7,500**.

After paying off the necessary closing costs and real estate commissions, your **net profit** on the sale comes to approximately **$325,000**.

Step 5: The Power of Compounding Success

In this perfect scenario, the story doesn't end there. Armed with your initial profits from the redeemed lien and the windfall from the property sale, you reinvest into even more tax liens.

- You buy **five more liens** at various interest rates, ranging from 10% to 15%, with each lien attached to properties that are just as promising as your first investment.
- Over the next two years, three of the properties are redeemed, netting you a steady stream of **interest payments** that add up to several thousand dollars.
- The other two properties go into foreclosure, and you now own not just one, but **two more high-value properties** at a fraction of their market price.

You've built a portfolio of **real estate and returns** that most investors can only dream of. What started as a single $7,500 tax lien certificate has ballooned into a **multi-property empire**, delivering annual returns of **10-15%** on interest alone, plus the added value of prime real estate holdings.

Step 6: The Freedom to Choose

In this perfect world, tax lien investing has given you the **freedom to choose your next steps**.

You can:

- Continue reinvesting in tax liens to compound your success.
- Sell your properties and enjoy a significant **cash windfall**.
- Hold onto the properties for **long-term rental income**, benefiting from rising real estate values and passive cash flow.

The possibilities are endless. Tax lien investing has given you the **financial flexibility** and **security** to create the life you've always dreamed of, all while maximizing returns and minimizing risks through careful planning, smart bidding, and well-timed investments.

Why This Perfect World Scenario Is Possible

What's inspiring about this scenario is that it's not just a pipe dream—it's **achievable**. There are incredible opportunities for those willing to put in the time and effort to understand tax lien certificate investing.

- **High returns:** Earning **10-18%** annual interest rates is common in many counties, and in some cases, even higher.
- **You can buy tax liens for a few thousand dollars, which is less than the market price.**
- **Secured investment:** Tax liens are secured by **real property**, reducing risk compared to many other forms of investing.

By learning how to research properties, understand bidding strategies, and predict outcomes, you can make your own perfect world scenario and build wealth through tax lien certificate investing.

— Chapter 3 —

A New Beginning

Marcus couldn't help but feel a mix of excitement and nerves as he pulled into the café where he was meeting James for the first time outside of their rideshare encounters. This was different—today wasn't just small talk in the backseat. Today, Marcus was about to step into a world he knew almost nothing about, but which had been on his mind ever since his first conversation with James.

He walked inside, spotting James at a corner table with his laptop open and a notebook next to his coffee. James waved him over with a friendly smile. "Ready for your first real lesson?"

"Absolutely," Marcus replied, sliding into the chair across from him.

As soon as Marcus sat down, James got straight to business. He pulled out a map and some printouts of auction lists. "Okay, Marcus. Today, we're going to start at the beginning—the front end of tax lien investing. You've heard the big picture of how this works, but before you can get to the perfect world scenario we talked about, you need to understand the groundwork. This is where the real work happens."

The Lesson Begins:
Understanding the Front End

James began explaining that tax lien investing isn't just about waiting for a return—it's about researching, preparing, and executing a plan. Marcus leaned in as James explained the key steps in the front-end process.

"You need to know how to research available tax liens, understand local laws, and perform due diligence on the properties you're interested in. Then, you have to register for auctions and develop a bidding strategy," James said, pointing at the checklist he had printed out for Marcus.

Marcus studied the sheet closely. "It sounds like a lot of work before you even make a bid."

"That's true," James agreed. "But the work you do on the front end is what sets you up for success. If you skip these steps or rush through them, you could end up overpaying for a lien on a worthless property."

James flipped open his laptop, showing Marcus an auction platform with upcoming tax lien sales. "Here's how you can research available tax liens. This is Maricopa County's auction site. Every county is different, but the process is generally the same."

Marcus watched as James navigated through the lists of properties, pointing out various details like delinquent tax amounts and property types. "You see here? You want to look for properties where the lien amount is a small fraction of the property's value. The bigger the difference, the better your chances of a good return."

The Importance of Due Diligence

After explaining how to access auction lists, James turned to the next step—due diligence.

"Here's where a lot of beginners mess up," James said. "You can't just rely on the auction site's information. You need to do your own homework. Look at the property's value, check its condition, and make sure there aren't any other liens or encumbrances on it."

Marcus was a little overwhelmed but grateful for the detailed guidance. James continued, "There are plenty of free tools out there, like county assessor websites and platforms like Zillow, that can give you a ballpark value. You can even drive by the property or use Google Maps to see if it's in good condition."

James pulled up a sample property from the auction list. "Let's say you're interested in this one. First, I'd check the property value online. Then, I'd see if there are any IRS liens or other complications. After that, I'd register for the auction."

Preparing to Bid

"Now let's talk strategy," James said. "Once you've done your research, you need to decide how much you're willing to bid. Set your limits early so you don't get caught up in the heat of the moment."

James explained how different counties use different auction formats, like bid-down interest rates or premium bidding. "In places like Maricopa County, competition can drive interest rates down, so you need to adjust your strategy depending on the auction format."

James demonstrated how to register on an auction platform and place a bid. "Make sure you understand the rules—every county has its own quirks. Once you place a bid and win, you have 24 to 48 hours to make the final payment and get your lien certificate."

Reflection

In this chapter, Marcus takes his first step into the front-end process of tax lien investing. James teaches him the importance of doing the work upfront—researching tax liens, understanding local laws, performing due diligence, and developing a bidding strategy. Marcus learns that while this process takes time and effort, it's the foundation for success in tax lien investing.

— Chapter 4 —

Front-End Overview for Tax Lien Investing In Maricopa County (Phoenix), AZ

Front-End Overview for Tax Lien Investing

This document provides a comprehensive checklist for tax lien investing, covering everything from researching available tax liens to successfully acquiring them at auction. The front-end process involves understanding local laws, performing property due diligence, registering for auctions, and developing an effective bidding strategy. By following this guide, you'll be well-prepared to maximize your investment opportunities while minimizing risks.

Key Sections:

Researching Tax Liens and Auctions:
Start by identifying counties that offer tax lien sales, accessing tax lien sale lists, and understanding the local laws governing tax lien investments. This lays the groundwork for finding high-potential properties and ensures you are compliant with state regulations.

Performing Due Diligence:
Once you have identified potential properties, evaluate their market value, inspect the property condition, and check for any other liens or encumbrances. This research helps you assess the risk and potential profitability of each lien.

Registering for Auctions:
Register with the county's auction platform, submit your bidder deposit, and review

the auction's terms and conditions. Proper registration allows you to participate in the auction process without any last-minute issues.

Developing a Bidding Strategy:
Set clear limits on how much you're willing to bid and determine the minimum interest rate you're comfortable with. An effective bidding strategy positions you to win profitable liens without overpaying.

Participating in the Auction:
Submit bids on the properties you've researched, ensuring your bids align with your predetermined limits. If you win a bid, promptly pay the balance and obtain the tax lien certificate.

Post-Auction Monitoring:
After the auction, track the redemption status of the liens. If the property owner redeems, you receive your investment plus interest. If not, you can begin preparing for the foreclosure process.

Estimated Costs:

- **Bidder Deposit:** 10-20% of your maximum bid amount.
- **Research and Due Diligence:** Costs for title searches, property condition assessments, and appraisals may range from **$100 to $500**.
- **Final Payment for Lien Certificate:** Due within **24-48 hours** after winning the bid, minus the deposit.

This **front-end overview** prepares you to navigate tax lien auctions effectively, guiding you from research and due diligence through bidding and post-auction monitoring. By following the steps outlined in the full checklist, you can confidently pursue tax lien investment opportunities and lay the groundwork for future profits.

Checklist for Front-End Tax Lien Investing
In Maricopa County (Phoenix), AZ

Step	Task	Description	Completed (Yes/No)
1. Researching Tax Liens and Auctions			
1.1	Identify Target Counties	Research counties that hold tax lien auctions, verify local laws, and understand historical performance.	☐
1.2	Access Tax Lien Sale Lists	Download tax lien sale lists from county treasurer websites or auction platforms like RealAuction.	☐
1.3	Review State and County Laws	Confirm tax lien laws, redemption periods, and interest rates in the chosen county.	☐
2. Due Diligence on Properties			
2.1	Research Property Values	Use county property assessor websites or real estate tools like Zillow to check property values and compare to lien amounts.	☐
2.2	Investigate Property Condition	Drive by properties, use satellite images, or check for code violations or environmental hazards.	☐
2.3	Check for Other Liens or Encumbrances	Conduct a basic title search to check for additional liens, such as IRS or mechanic's liens.	☐
3. Registration for Tax Lien Auction			
3.1	Register for the Auction	Register with the county treasurer's office or third-party platform (e.g., RealAuction).	☐
3.2	Pay Bidder Deposit	Submit a deposit (typically 10-20%) to participate in the auction.	☐
3.3	Review Auction Rules	Understand bidding rules, maximum interest rates, redemption periods, and auction formats.	☐

4. Developing a Bidding Strategy			
4.1	Set Bidding Limits	Determine the maximum bid for each property and the minimum acceptable interest rate.	☐
4.2	Evaluate Competition	Research how competitive past auctions have been and adjust strategy accordingly.	☐
4.3	Set Up Automated Bidding (if available)	Use automated bidding tools if the auction platform offers them.	☐
5. Participating in the Auction			
5.1	Place Your Bids	Submit bids based on your predetermined strategy and monitor real-time bidding.	☐
5.2	Manage Winning Bids	Pay the remaining balance (after deposit) within 24-48 hours if you win a bid.	☐
6. Post-Auction Due Diligence			
6.1	Track Redemption Status	Monitor whether the property owner redeems the lien within the redemption period.	☐
6.2	Prepare for Foreclosure (if necessary)	If the lien is not redeemed, begin preparations for foreclosure proceedings.	☐

Additional Notes:

- **Auction Platform:** Familiarize yourself with the specific platform used (e.g., **RealAuction**, **GovEase**) and its bidding mechanisms.
- **Set Up Alerts:** Set reminders or notifications for key auction dates, bidding deadlines, and payment schedules.
- **Adjust as Needed:** Always be ready to modify your strategy based on auction dynamics and competition.

Front-End Report for Tax Lien Investing

This report outlines the necessary steps and strategies for identifying, evaluating, and purchasing tax lien certificates. It focuses on the front-end of the investment process, helping investors navigate the research, registration, due diligence, and auction participation phases.

Step 1: Researching Tax Liens and Available Auctions

Before diving into the auction, it's critical to understand the market and identify available tax liens.

1.1. Identify Target Counties

- Choose counties that fit your investment strategy.

Counties such as Maricopa County, AZ, Miami-Dade, FL, and Cook County, IL are popular for tax lien investments but differ in processes and returns.

- Verify if the county holds tax lien sales (some counties sell tax deeds instead of liens).

Actions:

- Research state and county-specific tax lien laws and regulations.
- Look at historical redemption rates, interest rates, and bidding strategies in those counties.

1.2. Access Tax Lien Sale Lists

- Tax lien certificates are typically listed before the auction. Lists are available through:
    - County Treasurer's Office websites.
    - Third-party platforms like RealAuction or GovEase.

- These lists provide crucial details such as:
  - Property addresses, delinquent tax amounts, and property types (residential, commercial, vacant land).

Actions:

- Visit county websites or auction platforms to download the list of properties.
- Review past auction results to see how competitive the bidding tends to be.

1.3. Review State Laws on Tax Liens

- Each state has different rules on tax lien investing:
  - Redemption periods (e.g., 3 years in Arizona, 2 years in Florida).
  - Interest rates (e.g., Arizona offers up to 16%, Florida up to 18%).
- Confirm whether the state allows in-person or online bidding and any registration fees.

Step 2: Due Diligence on Properties

Once you've identified potential liens to bid on, conduct thorough research to minimize risks.

2.1. Research Property Values

- Estimate the value of the property relative to the lien amount. You want the lien to be a small percentage of the total property value.
- Use property appraiser tools such as Zillow, Realtor.com, or local county property assessors' websites.

Actions:

- Access the county assessor's database to check the current assessed value.
- Use online real estate platforms to compare the property's market value and surrounding neighborhood trends.

2.2. Investigate Property Conditions

- Physically visit the property if possible, or use satellite images (Google Maps, GIS tools) to inspect the condition.
- If the property is in bad condition (abandoned, damaged), you may end up owning it after foreclosure with costly repairs.

Actions:

- Check for code violations or environmental hazards via local government databases.
- Assess the neighborhood for overall property conditions, as they affect resale value.

2.3. Check for Other Liens and Encumbrances

- Conduct a basic title search to ensure no other outstanding liens or legal issues (like IRS or mechanic's liens) that might complicate foreclosure.
- Remember, tax liens are usually senior to most other liens, but certain liens (e.g., federal tax liens) could complicate the process.

Actions:

- Use county or third-party title search services to look for other liens or issues with the title.
- Ensure the lien is first in line for payment if the property is foreclosed upon.

Step 3: Registration for Tax Lien Auction

3.1. Register with the County or Auction Platform

- Most counties require bidders to register in advance, often online via platforms like RealAuction.
- You'll need to provide personal information, SSN/Tax ID, and proof of funds.

Actions:

- Register early through the county treasurer's website or the designated auction platform.
- Ensure you have the required documentation ready (SSN, deposit).

3.2. Pay the Bidder Deposit

- Most auctions require a deposit of 10-20% of your intended bidding amount.
- Deposits can be paid via ACH transfer or another approved method.

Actions:

- Submit your bidder's deposit to the county or auction platform before the auction begins.
- Confirm the deposit amount and payment deadline with the county.

3.3. Review Auction Rules

- Tax lien auctions have different rules, including bidding formats like bid-down interest rates or premium bidding.
- Familiarize yourself with key auction rules:
    - Maximum interest rate (e.g., 16% in Arizona, 18% in Florida).
    - Redemption periods and procedures.

Actions:

- Attend pre-auction workshops if offered by the county (some are available online).
- Read the auction terms and conditions provided by the county.

Step 4: Developing a Bidding Strategy

4.1. Set Your Bidding Limits

- Determine the maximum amount you're willing to invest in each property.
- Consider both the interest rate and potential property value if the lien is not redeemed.

Actions:

- Decide on a target interest rate and stick to it. Avoid overbidding, especially in competitive auctions.
- Prioritize properties with a high chance of redemption, but don't overlook lower-interest rate opportunities if the property has high resale potential.

4.2. Evaluate Auction Competition

- Understand how competitive the auction is:
  - In Maricopa County, competition may drive interest rates down to 8-10%.
  - In less popular counties, higher interest rates (closer to the max) may be easier to secure.

Actions:

- Track bidding patterns in prior auctions to adjust your strategy.
- Focus on properties where bidding interest is low, but the return on investment is still viable.

4.3. Use Automated Bidding Tools

- Some online platforms offer auto-bid tools that automatically adjust your bid if others outbid you.
- These tools help you stay competitive without constant manual bidding.

Actions:

- Set up automated bidding through the platform if available.
- Monitor real-time bidding to adjust your strategy as needed.

Step 5: Participating in the Auction

5.1. Place Your Bids

- Once the auction begins, place your bids based on your pre-set limits.
- Track the status of your bids in real-time through the auction platform.

Actions:

- Submit bids early to secure preferred interest rates or lien amounts.
- Monitor bids throughout the auction, adjusting if needed within your limits.

5.2. Manage Winning Bids

- If you win a lien, you will need to pay the remaining balance (minus your deposit) within a set period (usually 24-48 hours).
- The tax lien certificate will be issued to you once payment is confirmed.

Actions:

- Make your final payment via ACH or wire transfer.
- Obtain the tax lien certificate from the county as proof of your investment.

Step 6: Post-Auction Due Diligence

6.1. Track Redemption Status

- After the auction, track the redemption status of the properties. If a property owner pays their taxes, you will be refunded your initial investment plus interest.

Actions:

- Monitor redemption notices through the county's online portal or auction platform.
- Record interest payments and keep track of timelines.

6.2. Prepare for Foreclosure (if Necessary)

- If the lien is not redeemed during the redemption period, prepare to initiate foreclosure. This is covered in the back-end report.

Conclusion:

The front-end process of tax lien investing involves careful planning and due diligence. Following this step-by-step guide will help ensure you select the right liens, avoid costly mistakes, and secure profitable investments. Be sure to maintain a balance between thorough research and a well-thought-out bidding strategy to maximize your return on investment.

This front-end report complements the back-end report by covering everything from researching tax liens to securing a winning bid at auction. Together, they provide a comprehensive blueprint for tax lien investing success.

— Chapter 5 —

First Steps Into Investing

It had been a few days since Marcus and James met at the café, where Marcus had gotten his first real taste of the tax lien world. Since then, he had been thinking nonstop about how to begin his journey. The concepts James explained—the auctions, the research, and the strategy—felt within reach, but Marcus knew he needed to make one critical move: **take action**.

Today was that day.

Sitting in his living room, Marcus stared at his old laptop. The screen flickered occasionally, and its sluggish performance made the idea of investing online seem almost impossible. Frustrated, Marcus knew that if he was serious about stepping into this new world, he needed an upgrade. It was time to buy a new laptop—a small investment in himself before he could make any investments in tax liens.

He grabbed his keys and headed out.

The Investment in Himself

At the electronics store, Marcus surveyed the rows of laptops, each one boasting faster processors and better graphics than the last. He wasn't interested in gaming or editing videos—he just needed something reliable, quick, and efficient for research and auctions. After speaking with a store associate, Marcus made his choice. A sleek, budget-friendly laptop with solid processing power.

As he paid, Marcus felt a rush of excitement. This wasn't just a computer—this was his first real step into the world of investing.

On the way home, his phone buzzed. It was James.

"How's it going, Marcus? Any progress?"

Marcus smiled, glancing at the laptop bag in the passenger seat. "Yeah, I'm on my way home with a new laptop. I figured if I'm going to get serious about tax lien investing, I need the right tools."

"Good thinking," James said, clearly pleased. "You'll need that for research and for getting into the auctions. Speaking of which, how about we go over some next steps when you're ready?"

Getting Set Up

Back home, Marcus wasted no time setting up his new laptop. The speed was a world of difference from his old one, and it made him feel more confident in tackling what was next. As he logged on and opened up his browser, he realized how much information there was about tax lien investing. It was easy to feel overwhelmed.

That's when James called again.

"Alright, Marcus, ready for your next steps?"

"Yeah, let's do this," Marcus said, grabbing a notepad to jot down any important details.

"First, you need to decide which counties you want to target," James explained. "Remember what I told you—start with counties that have high redemption rates. You want your first investments to be easy wins, where the property owners are more likely to pay their back taxes and redeem the liens."

Marcus nodded, scribbling down notes. "High redemption rates. Got it."

"Next, start small," James continued. "Don't put all your money into one lien. With your budget, aim for lower-priced liens—maybe around $1,000 to $3,000. That way, you can spread your risk across a few properties."

Marcus wrote quickly, absorbing the advice. "So, I should look for a couple of smaller liens instead of one big one?"

"Exactly," James replied. "You're not looking to take ownership of properties just yet. You want your money back with interest, so focus on redeemable properties—owner-occupied homes, properties in decent neighborhoods. Stay away from anything that looks abandoned or is in bad shape."

Preparing for Auctions

"Now," James said, shifting the conversation. "Once you've done your research and found a few properties you're interested in, you'll need to prepare for the auction. Set your limits before you start bidding."

"Limits?" Marcus asked.

"Yeah. Decide the maximum amount you're willing to pay or the minimum interest rate you'll accept. Don't get caught up in a bidding war and overpay. Even a 10-12% return is a great rate compared to traditional investments."

Marcus wrote it all down: stay disciplined, set limits, don't overbid.

"And finally," James said, "when the liens redeem and you get your money back with interest, reinvest those funds into more liens. It's all about compounding your returns."

Marcus paused, pen hovering over his notepad. "So, it's really all about taking baby steps, right? Start small, learn the ropes, and keep reinvesting?"

"Exactly," James said. "You've got it. This is a long-term game, Marcus. You'll build confidence with each lien, and before you know it, you'll be ready to tackle bigger opportunities."

Marcus closed his laptop, feeling a sense of clarity and excitement. This was it—his first steps into investing. With James's guidance and his new laptop, Marcus was ready to start his journey.

Reflection

In this chapter, Marcus makes his first tangible step into the world of tax lien investing by investing in himself with a new laptop. He continues his mentorship with James, learning the importance of starting small, focusing on high redemption rates, and staying disciplined during auctions. The chapter sets up Marcus for his next lesson—growing his portfolio and building confidence.

— Chapter 6 —

From Baby Steps to Big Returns: A New Investor's Guide to Tax Lien Success

Entering the world of tax lien investing can feel overwhelming, especially if you have less than $10,000 to invest and don't have the resources for foreclosures or property management. But the good news is that you don't need to start big to succeed in this field. Even with a small amount of savings, you can earn **consistent returns** while minimizing risk, simply by focusing on **high-redeeming tax liens** that allow you to get your money back with interest.

This chapter provides a step-by-step strategy for new investors to safely enter the tax lien game, earn interest on their investments, and build confidence for future growth. With careful planning, strategic bidding, and the right approach, you'll be able to grow your capital while learning the ropes of tax lien investing.

Key Steps:

1. **Start in Counties with High Redemption Rates:**
   Focus on counties where property owners are more likely to **redeem their tax liens**, giving you a higher chance of getting your money back with interest. Counties with strong real estate markets and a history of high redemption rates are ideal for minimizing risk.

2. **Focus on Lower-Priced Liens:**
   With a budget under $10,000, it's best to invest in **smaller tax liens**, typically ranging from **$1,000 to $5,000**. This allows you to diversify your investments and

reduce the risk of holding a single, higher-value lien.

3. **Prioritize Redeemable Properties:**
   Target **owner-occupied homes** and properties in desirable neighborhoods where owners are motivated to pay off their tax debt. Avoid properties that are abandoned or severely damaged, as they are less likely to be redeemed.

4. **Bid Strategically at Auctions:**
   Set clear **bidding limits** before the auction, and focus on getting a fair interest rate without overpaying. Even a **10-12% return** is significantly better than many traditional investments, so stay disciplined in your bidding.

5. **Calculate Expected Returns:**
   Use an **interest calculator** to estimate how much you can earn from each lien based on the interest rate and redemption period. Factor in the possibility of early redemption, which could shorten the time you hold the lien but still deliver solid returns.

6. **Prepare for Redemption and Reinvestment:**
   Once the property owner redeems the lien, you'll receive your **initial investment back plus interest**. Reinvest those funds into new tax liens to compound your returns and build a growing portfolio over time.

Key Takeaways:

- **Start small, grow steadily**: You don't need large sums of money or a complex foreclosure process to succeed. Small tax lien investments can deliver excellent returns.
- **Focus on redemption, not foreclosure**: As a new investor, aim to earn interest and avoid taking ownership of properties through foreclosure, which can involve higher costs and risks.
- **Reinvest and compound your gains**: As you build confidence, reinvest your profits to grow your portfolio and capitalize on the power of compound returns.

By following this strategy, you can enter the tax lien market with confidence, earn consistent returns, and eventually grow your investments into larger opportunities.

From Baby Steps to Big Returns:
A New Investor's Guide to Tax Lien Success

Step	Task	Description	Completed (Yes/No)
1. Start in Counties with High Redemption Rates			
1.1	Research Counties	Look for counties with high redemption rates (85%+), indicating that property owners are likely to pay their back taxes.	☐
1.2	Target Counties with Growing Markets	Focus on counties with strong real estate markets and increasing property values to reduce foreclosure risks.	☐
2. Focus on Lower-Priced Tax Liens			
2.1	Set a Budget for Lower-Priced Liens	Aim to invest in tax liens with a value between $1,000 and $5,000 to spread risk and fit within your budget.	☐
2.2	Diversify Across 2-3 Liens	Consider purchasing multiple smaller liens rather than putting all your funds into one to reduce your risk.	☐
3. Prioritize Properties with Likely Redemption			
3.1	Research Owner-Occupied Properties	Focus on properties where the homeowner is likely to redeem the lien, such as owner-occupied homes.	☐
3.2	Avoid Problem Properties	Stay away from abandoned or heavily damaged properties that may be difficult to redeem or sell.	☐
4. Bid Strategically at Auctions			
4.1	Set Bidding Limits	Establish clear bidding limits based on the interest rate and property value, and avoid getting caught up in emotional bidding wars.	☐

4.2	Focus on Reasonable Interest Rates	Even if interest rates drop to 10-12%, this is still a great return compared to traditional investments.	☐
5. Calculate Your Expected Returns			
5.1	Use an Interest Calculator	Before bidding, calculate how much interest you'll earn based on the lien amount, interest rate, and expected redemption period.	☐
5.2	Factor in Early Redemption	Be prepared for early redemption, which could reduce your interest but still provide a solid return.	☐
6. Prepare for Redemption and Reinvestment			
6.1	Track Lien Redemption Status	Monitor the status of the liens you've purchased through the county or auction platform.	☐
6.2	Reinvest After Redemption	As soon as a lien is redeemed, reinvest your profits in new tax liens to compound your returns over time.	☐

Additional Notes:

- **Stay focused on redemption:** For new investors, the goal is to earn interest through lien redemptions rather than dealing with foreclosure.
- **Diversify your liens:** Spread your investments across multiple smaller liens to reduce risk and improve your chances of earning consistent returns.
- **Stick to your budget:** Never overextend yourself. The goal is to earn reliable returns while building confidence for future, larger investments.

From Baby Steps to Big Returns:
A New Investor's Guide to Tax Lien Success

If you're new to tax lien investing, have less than $10,000 in savings, and aren't ready to handle the costs of foreclosure or eviction, that's okay. The beauty of tax lien investing is that you can start with small investments that offer great returns without needing to take on the responsibilities of property ownership. You don't need to jump into the deep end right away—there are strategies designed for investors who simply want to get their money back with interest, build confidence, and grow their capital over time.

Let's walk through a strategy that will help you safely enter the tax lien game, minimize your risks, and gradually build the knowledge and resources you need to eventually play alongside more experienced investors.

The Goal:
Consistent Returns Without Owning Property

As a new investor, your focus should be on earning interest from tax lien certificates, not necessarily on foreclosing on properties or dealing with evictions. You want to:

1. Buy tax liens that are likely to be redeemed by the property owner, allowing you to earn interest on your investment without taking ownership of the property.
2. Avoid properties that require foreclosure or rehabilitation—those situations can tie up your funds and create additional financial responsibilities that may be difficult to manage with a small budget.
3. Build your investment portfolio over time with safe, small investments that compound into larger opportunities as your confidence and capital grow.

Step-by-Step Strategy for New Investors with Less than $10,000

Step 1: Start in Counties with High Redemption Rates

The key to earning interest on your investment without going through foreclosure is to target counties with high redemption rates. These are areas where property owners typically pay their delinquent taxes before the redemption period expires, meaning you're likely to get your money back with interest.

- **What to Look For:** Counties where redemption rates are 85-90% or higher, meaning that the vast majority of tax liens are redeemed before foreclosure is even a possibility. Counties with strong real estate markets, growing property values, and relatively low foreclosure rates are ideal.

Actions:

- Research counties in states like Arizona, Florida, or New Jersey, which often have high-interest rates and good redemption rates.
- Look for online tax lien auctions in these counties, many of which allow out-of-state investors to participate without needing to be physically present.

Step 2: Focus on Lower-Priced Tax Liens

Since your goal is to avoid foreclosure and simply earn interest on your investment, you can focus on lower-priced tax liens that are easily redeemable. Many tax liens are sold for amounts as low as $1,000 to $3,000, which means you can purchase multiple liens within your budget and spread your risk across different properties.

- **What to Look For:** Smaller liens on residential properties in desirable areas, where the homeowners are more likely to pay their back taxes. Avoid liens on vacant land or commercial properties, which can be more difficult to redeem.

Actions:

- Search for tax liens on residential homes with lower delinquent tax amounts, typically in the range of $1,000 to $5,000.
- Aim to purchase 2-3 smaller liens within your $10,000 budget to diversify your investments and reduce your risk.

Step 3: Prioritize Properties with Owners Who Are Likely to Redeem

You don't want to be stuck with a property that you don't have the resources to foreclose on, so it's important to prioritize tax liens on properties where the owner is likely to redeem. Some clues that a property is more likely to be redeemed include:

- Owner-occupied properties: Homeowners who live in the property are more motivated to pay off their tax debt to avoid foreclosure.
- Properties in desirable neighborhoods: Homes in growing or stable neighborhoods are more likely to be redeemed because the owners will not want to lose valuable real estate.

Actions:

- Research the neighborhoods and the condition of the properties behind the liens. You can use online tools like Zillow or county property appraisers to get a sense of property values.
- Avoid properties that appear to be abandoned or in disrepair, as these are less likely to be redeemed.

Step 4: Bid Strategically at Auctions

As a new investor, you'll need to bid strategically at tax lien auctions to maximize your returns. You don't need to aim for the maximum interest rate every time, but you do want to get a fair rate that will give you solid returns while keeping your risk low.

- **What to Look For:** Auctions that use bid-down interest rates (common in states like Arizona and Florida) can drive down the interest rate quickly, but don't get discouraged. Even if the final interest rate is 10-12%, this is still an excellent return compared to traditional investments.

Actions:

- Set your maximum bid based on the interest rate you're comfortable with. If the bidding goes too low, don't be afraid to walk away. There will always be more opportunities.
- Stay patient during the auction process. Focus on getting a reasonable rate for a good property, rather than getting caught up in emotional bidding wars.

Step 5: Calculate Your Expected Returns

Before you bid on any tax lien, it's important to calculate your expected returns so you know exactly how much interest you can earn and how long you may need to wait before the lien is redeemed.

- **What to Look For:** Most tax liens pay 10-18% interest, depending on the state. If you hold the lien for one year, this means you can expect to earn $100 to $180 for every $1,000 invested. If the lien is redeemed early, you'll still earn a prorated portion of the interest.

Actions:

- Use a simple interest calculator to estimate your returns based on the interest rate and the amount of time you expect to hold the lien.
- Factor in the possibility of early redemption. Even if the lien is redeemed in 6 months, you'll still earn a solid return without having to deal with foreclosure.

Step 6: Prepare for Redemption and Reinvestment

In this strategy, redemption is the goal. Once the property owner pays off their delinquent taxes, you'll receive your initial investment back plus interest. The best part? You can reinvest your profits into more tax liens, gradually building your portfolio and increasing your returns over time.

- **What to Look For:** Once you receive your redemption payment, you can immediately look for the next round of tax lien auctions to reinvest your funds.

Actions:

- Keep an eye on upcoming auctions in the counties where you've already had success. If you've done well in one county, it may make sense to continue investing there.
- As your portfolio grows, consider expanding into other counties with high redemption rates and solid interest returns.

Why This Strategy Works for New Investors

1. **Low-Cost Entry:** You don't need to spend tens of thousands of dollars or take on the risk of property ownership. With just a few thousand dollars, you can start earning interest on tax lien certificates.
2. **Low Risk of Foreclosure:** By focusing on high redemption rates and owner-occupied homes, you can minimize the likelihood that you'll have to foreclose on a property—a costly process that you may not be ready to handle.
3. **High Returns:** Even at lower interest rates, tax lien certificates offer much higher returns than most other investments. Earning 10-15% on a secure, low-risk investment is a great way to grow your savings.
4. **Compounding Success:** As you earn interest on your initial investments, you can reinvest those profits into more tax liens, allowing your returns to compound over time. With each successful investment, you're building toward larger opportunities and greater financial flexibility.

Building Confidence for the Future

This strategy is perfect for new investors who want to get a taste of the tax lien game without diving headfirst into more complex situations like foreclosure or eviction. By starting small, focusing on redeemable liens, and earning consistent interest, you'll build the confidence, knowledge, and capital needed to eventually scale up your investments.

Once you've built a track record of success and grown your portfolio, you'll be ready to take on bigger opportunities, including larger tax liens and potentially even foreclosures that can yield significant profits.

For now, your goal is simple: get in the game, earn your returns, and reinvest your profits until you're ready to run with the big dogs.

Final Thought:
You Can Get in the Game

Even with less than $10,000, you can start investing in tax lien certificates, earn high returns, and avoid the risk of foreclosure or property ownership. This strategy is designed to help you get your feet wet, build your investment confidence, and create a solid foundation for future growth. The best part? You don't have to wait—you can start today.

Tax lien investing is accessible, profitable, and an excellent way to build your wealth over time. Stick to this strategy, and soon, you'll have the resources and experience to scale up and explore even bigger opportunities.

— Chapter 7 —

The First Auction Experience

Marcus sat at his kitchen table, the new laptop humming quietly in front of him. His notes were scattered across the surface—everything James had taught him about bidding strategies, doing due diligence, and avoiding overpaying. Today was the day. It wasn't just talk anymore. Marcus was about to participate in his first tax lien auction.

The auction was online, and Marcus had already spent the morning doing some final checks on the properties he was interested in. He'd followed James's advice closely, looking for liens on owner-occupied homes in decent neighborhoods and setting a strict budget. His palms felt slightly damp as he logged into the auction platform, reminding himself to stay calm.

He had three properties in mind, each with liens valued between $2,000 and $3,000. His goal was simple: win at least one lien and, more importantly, not let the excitement of bidding drive him to make a poor decision.

The Auction Begins

The screen flickered as the auction countdown hit zero. Properties started appearing, one after another, and the bids started pouring in. Marcus's heart raced. He watched as some bidders seemed to get caught up in the competition, driving interest rates lower and lower—some as low as 5%.

Marcus knew he couldn't let that happen to him. "Stick to the plan," he muttered to himself, remembering James's advice: "Set your limit, and don't go over."

Finally, one of the properties he had marked earlier popped up. A modest three-bedroom house in a middle-class neighborhood. The lien was priced at just under $2,500. Marcus set his maximum bid and kept a close eye on the screen. Several other bidders were in play, but Marcus held steady, sticking to his minimum interest rate goal of 12%.

As the bidding slowed, Marcus's number remained the highest. A final bid flashed across the screen, and then… nothing. The auctioneer's hammer dropped virtually, and it was over. Marcus had won his first lien. He sat back, exhaling the breath he hadn't realized he was holding.

He had done it. He'd won the lien for a property with a redemption period of two years and an interest rate of 12%. Not only had he made his first real investment, but he had also done so without falling into the trap of overbidding.

The First Win

Later that evening, Marcus called James to share the news. "I did it," he said, his excitement palpable. "I won my first lien at 12%."

James laughed on the other end of the line. "Congratulations, Marcus! How does it feel?"

"Amazing," Marcus admitted. "I kept thinking I'd mess up or get too excited and bid too high, but I stuck to the plan."

"That's the key," James said. "The first win always feels good. Now, don't forget the next steps—make sure you've got the payment ready, and once it's processed, you'll officially own the lien."

"Got it," Marcus said, nodding, even though James couldn't see him. "What comes next?"

James paused for a moment. "Now, you wait. Either the property owner will redeem the lien and you'll get your money back with interest, or they won't, and you'll have the option to foreclose and take ownership of the property. In the meantime, you keep learning, keep researching, and maybe look for your next lien."

Marcus felt a rush of energy. He had taken his first step, and now he was hungry for more.

Reflection

In this chapter, Marcus takes part in his first tax lien auction. He successfully bids on a lien, staying disciplined and sticking to the plan James had laid out for him. This experience solidifies Marcus's confidence in the process, marking a major milestone in his tax lien investing journey.

— Chapter 8 —

One-Day Quick Start: 7 Action Steps to Begin Tax Lien Investing

If you're ready to dive into tax lien investing and want to get started in just one day, follow this simple, **step-by-step guide** to begin your journey.

Step 1: Educate Yourself on the Basics (1-2 Hours)

- **Learn the Fundamentals:** Spend some time understanding what tax lien certificates are, how interest rates work, and what happens if a lien is redeemed or foreclosed.
- **Resources:** Watch short videos or read quick guides online for a solid foundation.

Step 2: Choose the Right State and County (1-2 Hours)

- **Research States:** Look for states with high interest rates (10-18%) and short redemption periods.
- **Pick a County:** Select counties that offer online tax lien auctions for easy access. Popular options include Maricopa (AZ), Miami-Dade (FL), and Cook County (IL).

Step 3: Register for an Online Auction (30 Minutes)

- **Create an Account:** Visit your chosen county's website and register as a bidder.
- **Submit Documents:** Upload any necessary ID or documentation to complete the registration.

Step 4: Do Basic Due Diligence on Properties (1-2 Hours)

- **Review Auction List:** Identify properties with affordable liens (between $1,000 and $5,000).
- **Check Property Condition:** Use tools like Zillow or Google Maps to evaluate the property's location and condition.

Step 5: Set a Budget and Bidding Strategy (30 Minutes)

- **Define Budget:** Set your maximum investment limit (e.g., $2,000-$5,000).
- **Interest Rate Goal:** Aim for a minimum interest rate of 10-12%.
- **Prepare for Competition:** Stick to your budget and avoid overbidding.

Step 6: Participate in the Auction and Secure Your First Lien (1-2 Hours)

- **Place Bids:** Log in to the online auction platform and bid on 2-3 properties.
- **Complete Payment:** If you win, ensure payment is made within the required timeframe.

Step 7: Track Your Investment and Plan for Redemption (30 Minutes)

- **Monitor Lien Status:** Set reminders for the redemption period (usually 1-3 years).
- **Reinvest Profits:** Once the lien is redeemed, reinvest your earnings to grow your portfolio.

Stay Focused, and Follow the Steps...

By following this guide, you can quickly start your tax lien investing journey in one day, putting yourself on the path to earning interest income and potentially acquiring real estate through foreclosure. Stay focused, follow the steps, and reinvest your returns to steadily grow your investments.

One-Day Quick Start:
7 Action Steps to Begin Tax Lien Investing

Step	Task	Description	Completed (Yes/No)
Step 1: Educate Yourself on the Basics (1-2 Hours)			
1.1	Learn Tax Lien Investing Fundamentals	Watch videos, read blogs, and familiarize yourself with tax lien certificates, interest rates, and redemption periods.	☐
1.2	Review IRS or County Websites	Browse official websites for additional info on tax lien processes.	☐
Step 2: Choose the Right State and County (1-2 Hours)			
2.1	Research Favorable States and Counties	Look for states with high interest rates (10-18%) and counties with online auctions and high redemption rates.	☐
2.2	Pick a County to Invest In	Select a county that offers online auctions for easy access.	☐
Step 3: Register for an Online Auction (30 Minutes)			
3.1	Create an Account	Visit your chosen county's auction website and register as a bidder.	☐
3.2	Upload Documentation	Submit any required documents (proof of ID, tax forms).	☐
Step 4: Do Basic Due Diligence on Properties (1-2 Hours)			

4.1	Review Auction List	Identify lower-priced liens (e.g., $1,000-$5,000).	☐
4.2	Use Online Tools	Check property locations and conditions on Zillow or Google Maps. Avoid properties in disrepair.	☐
Step 5: Set a Budget and Bidding Strategy (30 Minutes)			
5.1	Define Budget	Set a maximum budget for your first investment (e.g., $2,000-$5,000).	☐
5.2	Establish Interest Rate Goal	Decide on a target interest rate (e.g., minimum 10-12%).	☐
5.3	Prepare for Competitive Bidding	Be ready to walk away if bids go over your limit.	☐
Step 6: Participate in the Auction and Secure Your First Lien (1-2 Hours)			
6.1	Log In to Auction Platform	Participate in the auction for the selected properties.	☐
6.2	Place Bids	Bid on 2-3 properties to increase your chances of success.	☐
6.3	Pay for Your Lien	Complete payment within 24-48 hours if you win a lien.	☐
Step 7: Track Your Investment and Plan for Redemption (30 Minutes)			
7.1	Set Reminders for Redemption Period	Mark the calendar for the lien's redemption period (typically 1-3 years).	☐
7.2	Monitor Lien Status	Stay informed of any redemption activity via the auction platform.	☐

Pro Tips:

- **Stick to Your Budget:** Set a bidding cap and avoid overbidding.
- **Focus on Owner-Occupied Homes:** These are more likely to be redeemed.

- **Reinvest Earnings:** Once a lien is redeemed, reinvest to grow your portfolio.

This checklist ensures you can get started with tax lien investing within one day, providing clear steps and checkpoints to guide your progress.

Starting your journey in tax lien investing doesn't have to take weeks of preparation. With focus and the right steps, you can begin the process in just one day. Here's a streamlined action plan to get you up and running quickly while laying a solid foundation for your future success.

Step 1: Educate Yourself on the Basics (1-2 Hours)

Before you invest, it's important to understand how tax lien investing works. Spend a couple of hours familiarizing yourself with the key concepts.

Key Concepts to Learn:

- What is a tax lien certificate?
- How do interest rates and redemption periods work?
- What happens if the lien is redeemed or foreclosed?

Resources:

- Watch a few short YouTube videos or read blog posts on tax lien investing basics.
- Browse the IRS or county websites for additional info on tax liens.

Step 2: Choose the Right State and County to Invest In (1-2 Hours)

Your next step is to pick a state and county where you'll invest. This will vary based on interest rates, redemption periods, and auction styles.

Action Items:

- Use online resources to research states with favorable tax lien laws (e.g., Florida, Arizona, New Jersey).
- Choose a county that offers online tax lien auctions so you can participate without needing to attend in person.

Quick Tips:

- Look for counties with high redemption rates (85%+) and interest rates between 10-18%.

Step 3: Register for an Online Tax Lien Auction (30 Minutes)

Most tax lien auctions are conducted online, allowing you to bid from anywhere. You'll need to register with the county or auction platform before you can participate.

Action Items:

- Visit the official website for your selected county or auction platform.
- Create an account and register as a bidder.
- Upload any required documentation (e.g., proof of ID, tax forms).

Pro Tip:

- Some counties require a deposit to register, so be ready with funds (e.g., $500-$1,000) for bidding.

Step 4: Do Basic Due Diligence on Properties (1-2 Hours)

Once you're registered, you'll want to evaluate properties in the auction to ensure you're making smart investments.

Action Items:

- Review the auction list and identify lower-priced liens (e.g., $1,000-$5,000).
- Use online tools like Zillow or Google Maps to quickly assess the property's location and condition.
- Avoid properties that appear abandoned or in disrepair.

Pro Tip:

- Focus on owner-occupied homes in stable neighborhoods to increase the chances of lien redemption.

Step 5: Set a Budget and Bidding Strategy (30 Minutes)

Determine your budget and establish a bidding limit before entering the auction to avoid overbidding.

Action Items:

- Set a maximum budget for your first investment (e.g., $2,000 to $5,000).
- Decide on your target interest rate (e.g., minimum 10-12%) and avoid bidding below this threshold.
- Be prepared to walk away if the bidding goes beyond your limit.

Pro Tip:

- Remember that even a 10% return on a tax lien is much higher than traditional investments like savings accounts.

Step 6: Participate in the Auction and Secure Your First Lien (1-2 Hours)

Now it's time to participate in your first auction! This is where you'll place bids and secure your tax lien certificate.

Action Items:

- Log into the auction platform at the scheduled time.
- Place bids on 2-3 properties to increase your chances of securing a lien.
- If you win, make sure to pay for the lien within the designated time (often 24-48 hours).

Pro Tip:

- Stay focused and avoid getting caught in a bidding war. Stick to your pre-set budget and interest rate goals.

Step 7: Track Your Investment and Plan for Redemption (30 Minutes)

Once you've secured a lien, your next step is to monitor the status of your investment and prepare for redemption.

Action Items:

- Set up a calendar reminder for the redemption period (usually 1-3 years, depending on the state).
- Keep track of any updates from the county or auction platform regarding lien redemption.

Pro Tip:

- If the property owner redeems the lien, you'll receive your investment back plus interest. If not, prepare to move forward with foreclosure.

Final Thought:
Celebrate Getting Started!

By following this quick-start guide, you'll be up and running as a tax lien investor in just one day. You've taken the crucial first steps toward building long-term wealth and generating steady returns. Now, it's just a matter of staying focused, reinvesting your earnings, and scaling your portfolio over time. Congratulations—you're on your way!

The Investor and the Driver
A Story of Wealth and Wisdom

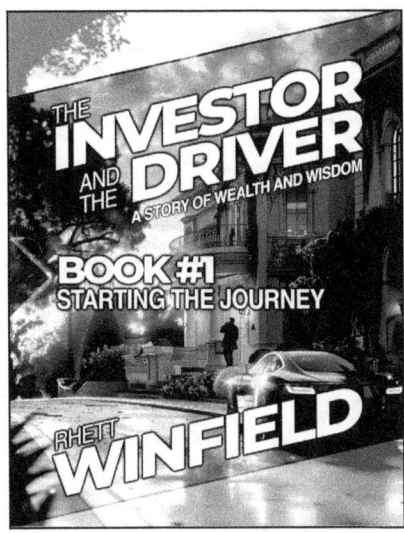

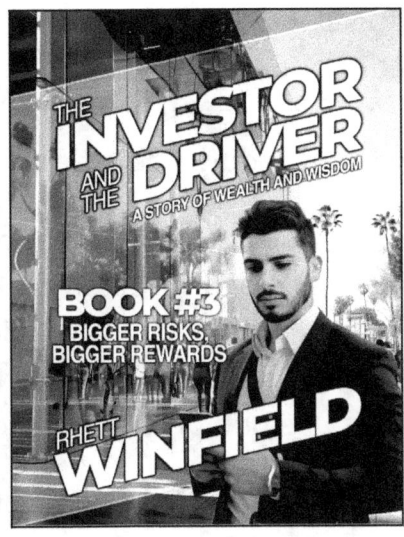

Book #1:
Starting the Journey

A successful investor needs to catch his next flight, so he requests a ride to the airport on his ride-share app. He's on the phone when he gets into the car, and the driver can't help but overhear the conversation.

Book #2:
Facing Challenges

James is the investor in our story who Marcus meets at the beginning. But James becomes much more than a successful investor when he decides to teach Marcus. He becomes a mentor. Everyone faces challenges, but this book is about the importance of having a wise and accessible mentor who truly helps you. James is that mentor in this story.

Book #3:
Bigger Risks, Bigger Rewards

Marcus, the driver at the beginning of the story in Book 1, is now a successful investor. He has learned his lessons well, and he has grown as a person. Book 3 brings him full circle in a way that will have you cheering for him because there will be a surprise realization and a new role for him at the end.

What comes next on Marcus's journey?

Marcus thought he had learned the ropes. But as he's quickly discovering, the world of investing isn't just about the numbers—it's about the person you become in the process.

The **Investor and the Driver** is more than a guide to financial success; it's a story of mentorship, resilience, and transformation. In this series, Marcus is taken under the wing of a seasoned investor, James, and step by step, he learns to navigate the opportunities and obstacles that come with tax lien investing.

A Journey Through Triumphs and Trials

From the excitement of a new beginning in **Book #1**, where Marcus first dips his toes into the world of investing, to the tough lessons in **Book #2**, where he faces the obstacles and ethical dilemmas that test his resolve, Marcus's path is anything but easy. Alongside his mentor James, Marcus learns that success is more than financial gain—it's about growing as a person, persevering through uncertainty, and making choices that define his future.

In **Book #3**, the stakes get even higher. Marcus is no longer the eager novice; he's a determined investor on the cusp of something big. But with new opportunities come greater risks. Every decision Marcus makes could either propel him forward or set him back—making it clear that success isn't just about money, but mastering life's ups and downs with courage and wisdom.

The journey isn't over yet.

Dive into the next installment and see where it takes you.

Learning Through Stories, Growing Without the Risk

What makes **The Investor and the Driver** series so unique is that it allows you to experience the highs and lows of investing without ever having to risk your own capital. By following Marcus's journey, you gain insights, strategies, and practical wisdom, all while safely navigating the complexities of investing through the perspectives of the characters.

This is the power of learning through story—Marcus faces the challenges, he makes the mistakes, and he reaps the rewards. As a reader, you get to absorb the valuable lessons without taking on the personal risks yourself. Whether it's understanding the nuances of tax lien investing or learning how to navigate the emotional and ethical decisions that come with it, this series equips you with the mindset and knowledge to grow.

And when you're ready, you'll be prepared to apply these lessons to your own life and investments, armed with the confidence of someone who has already experienced it—through the safety of a story.

— Epilogue —

Complications

Marcus sat at his desk, gazing at the latest update on his investment portfolio. It had been a whirlwind—just months ago, he was driving rideshare, barely scraping by, and now, here he was, watching his money grow in ways he never thought possible. James had been right all along—tax lien investing was real, and Marcus had found his stride.

But as he basked in his newfound confidence, something gnawed at him.

A ping from his phone broke the silence. It was an alert from the county clerk's office. One of the properties he had invested in—a seemingly small, safe bet—had an issue. The alert read: **"Notice of senior lien—immediate action required."**

His heart skipped a beat. Senior lien? How had he missed that? James had warned him about the dangers of senior liens, but Marcus had been so focused on his recent wins that he had barely considered the possibility.

He quickly dialed James, his mentor's voice calm on the other end.

"James," Marcus began, trying to steady his breath, "I just got a notice about a senior lien on one of my properties. What do I do?"

James was quiet for a moment. "Marcus," he said slowly, "this could get complicated. I told you about this. We're going to have to move fast—really fast."

Marcus's mind raced. Complicated? What did that even mean? Was his investment at risk? Could he lose everything he had worked for in a matter of days?

James's voice broke through his thoughts. "Look, meet me tomorrow morning at my office. We'll figure it out. But Marcus, listen to me carefully. This is the moment where things can either go very wrong or lead to something much bigger than you imagined."

The call ended, leaving Marcus staring at his phone. The comfortable rhythm he had fallen into was shattered. He thought he had it all figured out, but now, the reality of how quickly things could change hit him like a freight train.

As Marcus shut down his computer and turned out the lights, a sense of unease settled over him. He knew he was at a crossroads—one that could make or break everything he had built so far.

Tomorrow's meeting with James would change everything.

One way or another.

www.ingramcontent.com/pod-product-compliance
Lightning Source LLC
Chambersburg PA
CBHW062119220526
45471CB00010B/3796